REGIFTS

by Robert D. Grappel

Olympus Story House

List of Poems

Introduction

This is my second book of original poetry. The first one, GIFTS, was published nine years ago in 2007. As I said then, I seldom (if ever) sit down to write a poem intentionally. Poems come to me out of the blue – like presents in the mail from far-off friends. I can edit and polish them, rewrapping and refining the original idea, but the real source of the inspiration is always a mysterious gift. Sometimes it comes from interactions with friends and family, other times from my religious or musical families. Sometimes it comes during trips to far-off places, and other times during quiet moments. In this book I pass along these gifts to you. I hope you enjoy them.

Acknowledgments

This book contains quite a bit beyond poetry. The author would like to thank Frank Baker for his photographs accompanying the poem "Putting It Back In The Box", and Neal Walters for his photographs accompanying the poem "A Photograph of Heaven". Thanks to Ivan Stiles for his illustrations of "For Lucille", "Second Chances", "Looking Through Gauze Curtains", "The Name On the Door", "Missing the Mark", "Getting Off The Train", "Hannibal's Elephants", "A Losing Battle", "The Logic of Terrorism", "The Plastic Christmas Tree", "For Ivan", and "The Teacher". Last, but certainly not least, thank you to Teal Sallen for her artwork on "Whose Gift Is It, Anyway?", "Non-Newtonian Solids", "Baggage Charges", "Bon Voyage", "Looking Through Gauze Curtains", "Blenheim Cemetery", "A Losing Battle", "Bay of Naples", "Call and Response", "Finding the Third Way", "Death Without a Casserole", "My Eruv", "Quantum Scheduling" "Manzanar", "The Teacher", "Raw Materials", "The Plastic Christmas Tree", and "Dot the Dragon's Eye".

The author's photograph is by *Picture People*.

Thank you to Jessica Stambaugh for her assistance in the graphical design of this book.

The Cover

The cover of this book illustrates the poem "Manzanar". Translated from Spanish as "Apple Orchard", Manzanar was the site of a Japanese internment camp built in California during WWII. The background of the illustration is the actual plot plan of the Manzanar camp. The apple blossoms suggest the American aspect of this spot, while the cherry blossoms suggest the Japanese aspect. The irony is that apples are not native to America, nor are cherries native to Japan.

Bookends

This poem was inspired by a rabbinic commentary on the text of the Ten Commandments in the Bible.

The very first words of the Ten Commandments are:
"I am".
What could be more definite?
God exists,
And, thereby, the entire universe came into being.
The big question is answered,
We exist in a world that was created for a purpose.
What is that purpose?
Read on, dear friends.

The very last words of the Ten Commandments are:
"Your neighbor".
Nothing high and lofty here, But quite close to home.
We are each to be neighbors To God and to each other.
As Hillel taught,
"What is hateful to you, do not do unto others.
All the rest is commentary.
Go now, and study it!"

Whose Gift Is It, Anyway?

Thank you to Karla Armstrong, who inspired this poem.
You have been a gift to me for many years. Thanks, too,
to Teal Sallen for her illustration of this poem.

I drove to the store and parked my car.
I walked over to the candy aisle, and
Carefully inspected each box displayed there.
I thought about you.
The gift had to be large enough, special enough…
Beautifully wrapped and worthy
Of the love that I feel for you.

I wrapped the box carefully for mailing
And wrote your address clearly on the label.
I drove to the Post Office, paid the postage,
And sent you the package.
I thought about you on the way home.

A few days later, this gift appeared at your door.
You saw the return address on the wrapper
And smiled as you thought of me.
You took in this gift and removed the shipping box.
The colorful packaging
Giving hints of tasty treats within.
And, when you opened the gift box,
And tasted the deliciousness inside,
And felt the joy of friendship remembered,
You thought of me.

So…whose gift is it, really?
I paid for it.
You ate it.
I sent it out. You received it.
We, each of us, felt the warmth of love recalled.
So I guess we'll just call it a draw.

Second Chances

Thanks to Ivan Stiles for the illustration of this poem.

When Moses came down from Sinai carrying the
tablets of God's law,
The holy words engraved upon the physical stones,
He heard his people singing songs of jubilation
In their camp at the foot of the mountain.

They had gathered up their stores of precious gold
And made a tangible idol to worship,
A beautiful thing to see and touch,
To still their fears that Moses might never return
From the fiery mountaintop.

Moses flew into a rage beyond all controlling.
He threw down those precious tablets,
The Divine words shattered at his feet.
And Moses tore down the golden idol,
Broke it into pieces,
Burned the pieces in a furnace,
Mixed the ashes with water,
And made the people drink it.
The taste bitter in their mouths,
A reminder of the bitter years of slavery
They had so soon forgotten.
Then Moses went up a second time to Sinai.
He carved new stones and engraved again the words
That God had told him once before.

And when, at last, he came down from the mountain,
His face was radiant like the rising sun.

The people put those holy tablets in an Ark
To carry with them throughout their travels.
They wrote the words upon their hearts,
And became a light for all the nations.

The Bible never tells us what happened to those
broken tablets,
The fractured remnants of God's first teaching.
Did the people leave them in the desert?
Are they still out there, waiting for history to find?

The Rabbis teach that the people gathered up those
broken pieces
And placed them lovingly in the Ark – side by side with
the whole ones.
Wherever they went, those shards reminded them
Of their past failings and lack of faith at the foot of
Sinai,
And that God had let Moses go up the mountain
another time.

Our lives are not so different now
Though many centuries removed from the camp at the
foot of Sinai.
We, too, carry a load of broken pieces in our hearts,
Precious gifts we once had squandered,
Things of value that were neglected, Trifles we once had cherished,
And opportunities that were lost.

We are each a mingling of the broken and the whole.
Those shattered pieces help make us what we are.
The pain and loss, the memories and the longing
For what will never come again.
Yet even in our grief we must always remember

The greatest gift of all God's bounty
Was a second chance.

Non-Newtonian Solids

Classical physics separates all matter into three phases: solid, liquid, and gas. However, even those things that we regard as 'solid' will eventually flow – it just depends on the time-scale you choose to employ. Glass, ice, rock all flow if given enough time. The only constant is change. Thanks to Teal Sallen for her illustration.

Water flows
Sometimes smoothly without a ripple,
Or crashing wildly over rocks in its way.

Honey flows
Sweetly curling from a spoon above my teacup
In an amber wave, dissolving as I watch.

Tar flows
If the weather is hot enough,
Sticking to your shoes, leaving footprints on the road.

Glass flows
Slumping and distorting under gravity's steady urging,
Leaving a wavy prism where once was flatness.

Ice flows
In glaciers creeping inexorably down to the sea
Carving new features in the underlying rock.

Rock flows

A volcanic eruption births new land,
And tectonic plates mark its ending.

Star-stuff flows
Galactic gas merges to form a sun for a time
Then hurls new matter into the void.
Everything flows
You just have to wait long enough.

Dependent Nouns

Can you be a king by yourself? No, you require a nation
Who will acknowledge your sovereignty
And accept your leadership.
Only together with your people can you be a king.

Can you be a teacher by yourself?
No, without students to ask the questions
Your answers fall upon deaf ears.
Without a class to listen and to question
No learning will take place.

Can I be a husband by myself?
No, I am defined by the love of my wife.
Without the sharing and the caring...
The two lives spent as one entity...
I can only be half a man.

Baggage Charges

Sometimes even a cartoon on the Internet can inspire a poem! Thanks to Teal Sallen for her illustration.

Imagine that,
If every time you went out into the world,
You were charged a fee for all your emotional baggage.

Each slight remembered,
The harsh words once said in anger,
The cries of pain that went ignored,
And friends now faded away.

You'd have no room left in your carry-on bag
For pleasant memories
And encouragements, For sweet words
And gifts of love, freely given.

So, remember that
We are each allowed one "personal item"
As we travel on through life.
There is no fee for a case of kind thoughts
Or injuries left behind.

"Bon Voyage"

This poem was inspired as the first cruise ship I've ever been on set sail from Miami, Florida, for a week of sun and fun in the Caribbean. Thanks to Teal Sallen for her beautiful illustration.

The Miami skyline shimmers in the afternoon sun.
Pastel-color hotels cascading down the ocean's edge
Casting their tall reflections at the waterline,
While giant steel structures streamlined into the wind
Strain against the ropes that tie them to the land.

A momentary shiver…a low, rumbling throb.
Slow, almost imperceptible motion against the
background sky.
Buildings recede into misty shadows
As though seen through a wide-angle camera lens.

A strip of dark water forms below us
And shifts along the receding shore.
We have become part of sea and sky
No longer tied to Earth and home.

The Merits of Study

I must have read this passage of Talmud in the prayer book hundreds of times from my seat in the choir, but this morning it finally became clear to me in this poem. I guess that it takes a lot of repetitions for me to finally learn something new.

There are lots of commands in the Bible.
Hundreds of "thou shalt's" and "shalt not's."
So many chances for us to fail
Or miss something important.
It seems too daunting to even try.

So our Rabbis explained it in a simpler way.
The commandments are an investment in our future.
They are opportunities to practice good habits
And to feel the little successes that bring joy.
We can appreciate the benefits of a Godly life today,
But the principal remains throughout all the generations.

Honor thy father and thy mother:
Each of us may become, God willing, a parent some day.
We'll need to remember how we felt as children.
How it was to rely on someone beyond us for food and love.
When we looked up physically and emotionally to another.
When we recognized our own place in the world.
We need to get in some test runs – some rehearsals
Before we'll know how to honor God as adults.

Perform deeds of loving-kindness:
When we show kindness to another, we are reminded
Of how good it feels to experience kindness.
How each good deed reinforces the memories
Until doing kindness to others brings the same joy
As having another be kind to us.

Attend the house of study punctually, morning and evening:
No other divine commandment instructs us to be on time,
Perhaps because it's so hard to make time in our lives for learning.
We need to make the love of discovery such a joy
That we rush to meet it every time.

And, why twice – at the beginning and end of each day?
We recall that study isn't the end result.
It's the process.
We must fill our days with the work and the growing
In the directions that our study has shown to us.

Show hospitality to strangers:
Remember what it is like to be a stranger
Standing outside a comfortable group.
We are commanded to reach outside ourselves,
Beyond our parents, our families,
Our towns, our countries,
To encompass all people
Especially those not like us.

Visit the sick:
We must recall that we,
Or someone close to us, will face illness.
We should remember how that feels.
How helpless, how apart
The lack of control, the "why me?"
We need to rehearse the steps of life's dance
With someone not quite so close and personal
So that, when our time comes,

We'll be comfortable with the music.

Help the needy bride:
We should recall our joyous times.
Remembering how good they felt,
How we walked on clouds.
Such a gift we can give to others
And share our happiness with them.

Attend the dead:
No matter how we try, each of us will reach an ending.
Everyone around us, near or far, will not last forever.
This thought should not frighten us to inaction,
Instead, spur us to best use our lives for good.
It's our investment in the future.
Our chance to increase the stockpile
That will pay dividends to our future.

Pray with devotion:
Pray, because it exercises our emotional selves.
To stretch beyond our selfish limits
Into a larger space where God is waiting to meet us;
To enlarge our ability to feel the pain of others,
And to widen the circle of those we can love.

Make peace between individuals:
Why "individuals" when the world is filled with strife
Among nations and regions, religions and parties?
Perhaps because stopping a war is too difficult a challenge
For just one person to contemplate.
We're still having trouble with the "hospitality to strangers" idea.
So, we are instructed to make it personal,
Just deal with that person next to you.
For, when each individual is at peace with his neighbor,
All wars will end, and we'll need no further commandments.

Looking Through Gauze Curtains

This poem came to me during my recovery from cataract surgery. It's amazing how much loss we can adjust to if the process is gradual enough. Thanks to Ivan Stiles and Teal Sallen for their illustrations of this poem.

I've been looking at the world through gauze curtains
Years of indistinct shapes and muted colors.
My focus narrowed over time
Field of view limited
And restricted to the very near.

Yet all this changed in one brief hour.
The amazing vivid blue
Of the fluorescent lights in the recovery room.
The experience – for the first time in 50 years
Of reading clearly without thick glasses.
Literally seeing life through new eyes.

So, treasure every moment in the light.
Each sensation and opportunity to see
The world as it is, without blinders
Applied by time or by lessening of oneself
To see clearly what is all around you.

The Antique

"You should never refinish antique furniture."
I'm sure you've heard this advice.
"You'll reduce its value considerably."
Did you ever wonder why this is so?

Do we value every scrape and dent,
Each crack and stain and blemish,
The faded colors and the dirt?
A new finish would be much smoother,
More even, clear and shiny.
So, why not strip and re-varnish
That old antique?

We cherish an antique for the life it's lived,
For the history it's seen,
And the events it recalls.
We cherish the reminder that it gives.
For though the "new" is ever with us,
What has value is that which endures
Through time and nature's challenges
Like a treasured antique.

Eleven Questions

When a person reaches that 'certain age' (this poet already has), he starts to think about the time when his mental and physical abilities will start to wane. This poem was inspired by the "Mini-Mental State Examination (MMSE)" that is administered to detect the early stages of dementia.

What is the season?
What is today's date, day, month, year?
If your reply is "who cares!"
That's depression, not dementia.
Give yourself five points
If you get all the answers right
And an extra point if you add
"And it's another lovely day".

Where are we now?
State? County? Town?
Hospital? Floor?
Thankfully,
I can't answer those last two questions.

"Take the paper in your right hand,
Fold it in half,
And put it on the floor."
What if I'm left-handed? Do I lose a point?

"Please count backward from 100 by sevens."
For this I got a PhD in physics!

"Make up and write a sentence about anything.
The sentence must contain a noun and a verb."
"Life is a death sentence" qualifies.

"Show the patient two simple objects,
Such as a wristwatch and a pencil.
Ask the patient to name them."
Do I lose points when I reply
"Casio" and "PaperMate"?
Or, am I just being too literal?

So, for now, I pass the test of sanity.
And you do too, by reading this.

Seattle Autoharp Week

Sambica Camp, September 2007

When those of like minds gather
To share good songs and laughter
To tune our hearts in joyful chorus
And begin the task before us.

From far away and near we've come
To learn new licks, a chord, a strum
To share with others what we know
And gain from them a chance to grow.

In quiet evening, dreams may run
Before the setting of the sun
The harp strings of our souls now ringing
God hears the echoes of our singing.

For Lucille – A Congratulatory Ode

Bryan Bowers says that you must be able to play a tune perfectly three times in a row before you can claim that you really know it. In that case, Lucille Reilly's unprecedented third Mountain Laurel Autoharp Gathering championship is proof that she has gone well beyond "knowing it" to having all of us other players of the instrument acknowledge it too – hence this poem. Also, thanks to Ivan Stiles for his illustration.

To play a tune perfectly one time might be a fluke,
A comet's flash,
Blind luck,
A "one-hit wonder".

Nail it a second time and we're talking about skill,
Excellence,
Technical ability, Artistry.

But do it again a third time…
We've gone beyond just playing the tune
To creating magic in this listener's ear,
And joy in this poet's heart.

We other players pinch and strum,
Pluck and pick as well we can,

And furrow our brows in concentration
For the 'hard parts'.
Lucille does a fairy-dance upon the strings
With a sly smile that says
"Look, Ma – no hands!"

The Name On The Door

This poem was written while our dear Aunt Gertrude was living out her last days in a nursing home. She lived a very long and fulfilled life, but the end came in a slow and agonizing process. Thanks to Ivan Stiles for his illustration of this poem.

A sign on the wall announces,
"Today is Saturday",
"The season is winter – The next holiday is…"
Time moves slowly here
Congealed
No outside light invades.
Day or night, it's all the same.
Even the movie show is old
Bing Crosby, who never ages.

A parade of the same dull faces
Stalks this length of corridor
To the rhythm of repeating wails,
And a ringing telephone.
The staff maintain their ordered rounds
While the TV in the communal room keeps watch.

Until, one day, for good or ill,
Nature's balance tips slowly backwards…
Time restarts for one brief moment…
And they take your name off the door.

Today Is
Saturday

A Photograph of Heaven

This poem was written during a visit to the amazing Sagrada Familia Cathedral in Barcelona, Spain. Under construction for much more than a century, its amazing architecture instills awe and wonder among all who see it. Thanks to Neal Walters for the photographs.

I stood in the nave of "La Sagrada Familia"
Stone columns reaching heavenward
Two hundred feet to form arches above my head.
Organic forms
Like a grove of cypress trees
In a green cathedral
In a Barcelona park
Or like the cedars of Lebanon
From Solomon's Temple.

This place has been growing for 150 years.
It's still not done growing.
A century is a long time for a man,
But not so long for a tree.

Light pours in through the stained-glass walls:
Blues and greens from the "Passion" side
Like glimpses of sky through a leafy canopy
Bright yellow from the "Nativity" side
Like the sunrise of a new day
And orange from the last remnants of a sunset.

Organ chords echo from the walls
And give their cues to angel choirs
Lurking above the lofts.

At the altar,
A group of tourists raise their cellphones up
To capture bits of heaven through a tiny lens,
To hold the images of creation
In the palm of their hands.
But I choose to use only my senses and my mind
To keep this brief moment
That God has given me.

Sherrie's Wine

I wrote this as a song in 1970 in the throes of my first "true love". The rhymes are not perfect, but I still feel this poem intently. I wonder where she is today...

Her face is moving swift, outside my window,
Running free.

She's running 'cross the silence
Of the night down to the sea,
And while I only paused a moment,
In that moment she was gone,
And I'm left with quiet loneliness
And this song.

How I long to taste the sweetness that was her life
When I met that face in misty morning,
Early in the light.

Little thought I had beginning
In those days so lost in time...
Of a glass of Sherrie's wine.

Now her memory shouts inside my head,
Resounding in the din.
"If a tree grew in the forest?"
Is the prize enough to win?

When I stop to pay the penalty

She rushes from my sight,
And in darkness, I am blinded
By the presence of the light.

But the loss is not enough to bear,
I cannot find the words
To tell you what I'm feeling
And the image that occurs

So please just reach inside yourself,
I'm sure there's something there.
Perhaps a glass of Sherrie's wine.

And suppose I was born yesterday
Could I leave the past behind?
Would I waken, screaming, in the night?
Going home, going home!

When we must, we join the shadows
That sing after the rain.
Who revel in the drowning, the baptism in the pain.

    And if I had twenty-one years to go a-wandering.
    Would I find the time to still the ache again?
    Or would life save me the bother to end it all within
    A glass of Sherrie's wine?

Questions

There is a story told about a student who has spent years in diligent study concerning the laws and observances of Jewish life. However, he was still bothered by many unanswered questions. Why does the world appear as it does? Why does God permit evil to exist? Why can't we all live peacefully? The student summoned up his courage to ask these questions of his rabbi. The rabbi answered, "Those are such wonderful questions. Why do you wish to trade them in for answers?"

The centerpiece of the Passover Seder is a set of four questions
Ritually asked by the youngest person present who is able to ask.
They are sung to a lilting melody that belies their depth
and meaning.
Their importance has transcended centuries.

Why is this night different from all other nights?
What makes this celebration worthy of such ritual and ceremony?
Special foods and lavish preparations?
Despite a history marked with remembered pain and trouble
From Egyptian slavery to Holocaust,
Plagues and pogroms in many lands,
Persecutions and unmarked graves
We yet remain to reach this season
Able to share a Passover meal
In relative ease and comfort.

The Seder also includes a set of four sons,
Each of whom has a question.
"What does this mean to you?"

"Why bother?"
"Why?"
And the unasked question.

While the rest of the Seder dutifully seeks to answer
these questions,
It is, perhaps, more important to keep asking more
questions.
Why, when we can enjoy a special meal, are there still
those who are hungry?
When we open our door for Elijah, why are there still
those without homes?
And, as we recline at ease and sing songs, why is so
much of the world still at war?

Maybe the real lesson of the Seder is that we are, each of us,
The son who "doesn't know how to ask".

Things I Don't Understand

Often, in fields as seemingly unrelated as physics and religion, we must employ techniques and tools that we don't really understand to reach 'truth'.

I don't understand quantum mechanics.
I can think about it with physical models and analogies
But I never feel it solidly 'in my gut'.
An electron is sometimes a particle
And sometimes a wave…
What is it, really?
I can solve equations to determine its properties
But what it is – I haven't a clue.
I can get to the 'right answer'
Without a real understanding.

The Old Testament lists 613 commandments.
I don't understand the meaning and value of each one.
Some seem contradictory
And some seem outdated.
Centuries of Rabbinic commentaries have sought
To explain and motivate each one.
To give us the "why" behind the action,
The rationale behind the command.
However, by performing the proper actions,
I can live a 'righteous life'.

Deuteronomy 11

The Bible says,
"You shall bind these words as a sign upon your arm".
It sounds pretty weird at first,
But wait a moment…
My friend wears a Patriot's jersey
To show his pride in our hometown team.
Another friend sports his University of Michigan sweatshirt,
And his daughter has a friendship bracelet.

The Bible continues,
"You shall make them a sign before your eyes."
Like Sandy's Yankee cap With its big blue 'Y',
The symbol of his favorite baseball team.

"You shall write them on the doorposts of your house"
At the last election
My neighbor put up a political sign in his front yard
To show us all which party he believes in.
I had a sign in my yard
Indicating which landscaping company I prefer.

"And on your gates."
There are many signs as you drive into our neighborhood:
"Entering Concord", "School Zone", "Town Center",
"Historic Area", "Conservation Land".
Our world is full of signs
Which remind us of important things.
Things we treasure, things we respect,
And things we want the world to know.

Wrestling With God

Thank you, Rabbi Mintz, for inspiring this poem. Yes, I was listening to your sermon this morning!

There can be great meaning in a nation's name.
You may learn a lot from what people call themselves,
The identity they select and cherish.

'Israel' means, "he wrestled with God".
Not for us Islam's submission,
'Insha'Allah' – "all is God's will".
Nor do we look to Christianity's "second coming"
When the world will be changed for us.

God told Abraham, the Bible says,
To sacrifice his son, Isaac,
As proof of his devotion,
Yet verses later God says "do not kill him."
Which is it?
Can even God be inconsistent?

We are filled with questions,
With doubts and nagging insecurity.
There is so much we do not understand,
And so many ways to see the world.
There are so many things that need fixing
And so many challenges along the way.

And... so we wrestle with our flaws and failings,
With our inability to know with certainty
What is good and true.

Yet, while wrestling is a contest
With winners and losers,
Pain and injury,
Scars and twisted knees,
It is the only sport that may include a hug.

Blenheim Cemetery

This poem came to me during a tour of the Jewish sites on the island of Curacao. Arriving from our cruise ship in the Caribbean, we viewed this oldest Jewish cemetery in the Americas, totally surrounded by an oil refinery – truly an unusual combination of sights and smells. Thanks to Teal Sallen for her collage.

The oldest Jewish cemetery in the New World
Lies fading in the bright Caribbean sun
On the island of Curacao.
Marble slabs, centuries old,
Crumble into the gravel paths
As we walk about
And look down at the cruise ships
Anchored in the port of Willemstad.

All around us loom the pipes and stacks
Of the Isla oil refinery.
Petroleum pervades the air.
Intruding on the peace and solemnity Of this historic place.

Yet, it's oddly fitting
This combination of oil and grave markers.
For what is oil but the remains of ancient plants and animals
Which died here long before history began?
The refinery is, in a way, their 'tombstone'.
Oil is but liquid life ready to be re-cycled,
Like the Jewish community on Curacao
That has survived here over so many generations.

In the distance, the flares of gas vents glow,
Plumes of orange flame rising like giant candles
Above the refinery stacks.
They cast an 'eternal light' on the grave markers
As we tourists walk with bowed heads
In this sacred place.

The Chosen

"The children of Israel shall be to Me a chosen people."
That sounds a bit like boasting,
Yet, I suppose that depends on what
We were chosen for.
If I were picked out of a police line-up
As the one who had committed a terrible crime,
That would not be a good thing.
When the principal made an example of me
But "all the other kids did it too!"
I wasn't very happy.
And, when I was eligible for the draft,
Being "selected" was not what I wanted to be.

"You shall be a nation of priests."
Most of us don't want to stand out very far.
We want to think "they're really just like us!"
If a hero has a fall from grace…
And even the most loathsome criminal
Gets his moment of fame.

"I shall make of you a great nation."
"Great" does not necessarily mean "numerous".
Just one individual can do great things.
An inspired soul with flaming passion
Can succeed where millions fail
And never even notice it.

"You shall be a light to the nations."
Does that mean a blazing flare far off and alone in the heavens?
Even the sun cannot remove darkness from the night,
And the moon may block its light from our view, if only
for a moment.
Better to walk among all the peoples of the Earth,
Each of us carrying our own lantern.

Why The Rain?

The prayer book says:
"You cause the wind to blow and the rain to fall"
While meteorologists speak of cold fronts and cumulus clouds
And physicists calculate the phase transitions of air and water.

Primitive peoples saw their gods as "super-humans"
Breathing storms out over their ships,
Hurling down thunderbolts upon their heads,
Sweating the dew and crying raindrops.

In ancient Greece, nature was seen in four elements.
Fire: the sun, heat, light, the motive forces
Earth: stability (the "bedrock")
Air: origin of spirits and chaotic change
Water: source of life

Philosophers bound these elements together within logic
A "natural order" both knowable and determined
Obtainable through human thought.

Modern science has brought many more elements to the table.
Mathematics can bring powerful tools to bear.
We see a dance of atoms and electrons
Where once there was only mist and fog.

Yet in the quiet peace after a summer storm is past
And golden sunlight once more paints the sky
What else can we "mere mortals" say but
"Thank You for Your miracles"

Times Square, New York City

This poem had its origin as Lynda and I were walking among the crowds near Times Square in New York. We were going to buy tickets to see a show – but the city was a show in itself.

The city throbs and roars
Full of nervous energy
Like a caged animal
Pacing back and forth in its cage,
Tail twitching.

Taxis honk and screech
Barkers tout their bargains into the din
While neon billboards flash
Against gray concrete And a drizzly sky.

A thousand conversations
With few listeners
As we line up at the ticket booth
To make our day's decision
And walk on.

Crash! Slam!
An accident on the next corner
Draws a small crowd.
Magnetism draws us to look
And wonder.

There are no sirens this time
No prone bodies,
No blood.
Just broken plastic
Added to the gutter trash.

So, we walk on.
The sky brightens and the sun appears.
Soon, we'll reach our theater…
Enjoy some hours of pleasure…
Then rejoin the world.

Relativity

This poem compares the relative worth of a baseball player in the overall "scheme of things". I can't hit home runs like Manny Ramirez, but can he write poems?

When Manny has a great season for the Sox
He'll bag more than two hundred hits.
The Boston fans will cheer
And the team will pay him twenty million plus,
A hundred thousand dollars a hit.

Eight poor families survive
In the projects of south Roxbury
Struggling to make a living
Below the poverty line.
Are they worth as much as one Manny single?

Is each Manny double the equal of three
Harvard students?
Does each homer have the merit of four grade-school teachers?
A fireman, a city-counsel member, or a bus driver?
All of them "most valuable players".

A Losing Battle

This poem was inspired by Rabbi Mintz's sermon at Rosh Hashonah (New Year) services today (9/26/2014). Achieving success is not so important as choosing the right things to strive for. Thanks to Ivan Stiles and Teal Sallen for their illustrations of this poem.

Moses strove to make the Israelite people a kingdom of priests
A light to the world, a holy people.
He failed.

Joshua fought to bring the entire land of Palestine together.
He failed.

Jeremiah sought to return the nation of Israel to justice
and right.
He failed.

Jacob wrestled all night with an angel
And came out of it with a limp.

God told Abraham to count the stars in the sky
An impossible task.
God knew that it was impossible,
And Abraham knew that it was impossible,
Yet he started counting.

Then God told Abraham
His children would be like the stars

Not an uncountable multitude,
But a nation of big dreamers.
Small in numbers, but large in goals
Unafraid to try – unafraid to fail.
Willing to start without seeing the finish line.
Willing to plant so that others would taste the fruit.
A people with this motto:
"The difficult we do today.
The impossible might take a little longer."

Fields of Greatness

This poem was inspired during a tour of the Gettysburg battlefield. I was struck by how "normal" the site appeared, even as our guide described the significant events that occurred here on those 3 days in July of 1863.

It doesn't look like much at first.
A few miles of gently sloping open land
Rising to a rounded hill
Framed by split-rail fences and a fieldstone wall.
Just a modest day hike on a sunny summer's day
From a sleepy farming town in Pennsylvania.
Even the famous names here are prosaic:
"The Wheat Field", "The Peach Orchard",
"The Angle", "Little Round Top".

Our guide leads us up a path to the hilltop,
The ground still wet from a morning storm,
And we try to imagine the clouds of acrid smoke,
The roar and whistle of shot and shell,
The rousing cheers and the anguished screams,
The moans and the deathly silences
Of those three days in July.

No general ever planned to come here.
The armies of North and South were each
On their way to somewhere else.
Yet here they met, and the world was changed forever.

As children we memorized
"Four score and seven years ago…"
Visualizing some great heroic image on a movie screen.

Yet the reality of it here seems far too small and commonplace,
Just a grassy field studded here and there with monuments
To remind us that one cannot plan for greatness.

We can only hope to be ready
When the chance for significance occurs.

We Have Today

I wrote this as a song many years ago (so it rhymes). The musical version has appeared on two CD's since then. The second verse was used as a chorus in the song.

I know not what tomorrow may unfold,
Or where the road as yet un-trod may lead,
While time and tide move onward ever bold
With no cessation in their daily speed.

We have today, with four and twenty golden hours
Reflecting moments that await beneath the sky, divine.
And this is mine to cherish as we wend our way
With thanks to God for giving us today.

The yesterdays I cannot re-adorn,
And bygone years I never can re-live,
While future happenings lie still as yet unborn,
But now is ever here with much to give.

We may not know the number of our years,
Or what the wanderings of our lives may bring.
So, let our faith prove stronger than our fears
To hail God as our savior and our king.

On Mice and Men

This is an old poem of mine written back during the period of the Cold War.

Hurry, scurry, little mouse
Beware the eyes of cat and owl
Who prowl shadows damp with death.
Beware the snapping monster's jaws
Lying in the basement.
Beware!

Flee to safety, singing bird
Beware the claws of cat and owl
Who wait in shadows damp with death.
Beware the lead projectile's flight
Leaping from the ground below.
Beware!

Hurry, scurry, little man Beware the beasts and men
Who left shadows damp with death.
Beware the deadly radio dust
Raining down from falling skies.
Beware, little man!

Call And Response

"Call and Response" is a common Western musical form where the singers and/or instrumentalists share the lead back and forth between them. "Call and Response" (or its fancier name 'antiphony') is pervasive in all sorts of music from classical to blues, rock-and-roll to jazz and gospel. Thanks to Teal Sallen for her illustration of this poem.

The central prayer of the Jewish liturgy, the 'Shema',
Consists of just six words in three short phrases.
It's an odd sort of prayer…
It doesn't sing God's praises
Or plead for forgiveness.
It neither asks for Divine favor
Nor seeks that which we cannot understand.

"Hear, O Israel!"
That's God talking.
OK, you've got my attention.

"The Lord is our God"
Why "our" instead of "your"?
This is humanity responding to God's call.
Creation is to be a partnership…
A duet between us and the One
Who calls upon us all to 'hear'.

"The Lord is one".
A direct statement

No distractions!
We cannot sing our part in Life's great song
Unless we first listen to the other's voice.
Yet – why must God ask us to hear?

Even amid the earthquake and thunder of the storm
The roaring winds and the tossing waves
We need the constant reminder
To listen before we begin to sing.

Putting It Back In The Box

Once each year, the "Mountain Laurel Autoharp Gathering" (MLAG) materializes, as if by magic, at the Little Buffalo Campground in Newport, Pennsylvania. For a glorious four-day period each June, autoharp players gather here from around the world to celebrate our instrument, the music, and the joys of shared fellowship. Thanks to Frank Baker for the photographs.

Just a windowless corrugated metal building
Standing at the edge of a Pennsylvania park.
Concrete floor newly-painted
It might seem a small factory or a warehouse.
Most of the year it's a site for campers and picnics,
Swimmers and hikers in the green Newport woods.

Then the trucks pull up outside,
The volunteers assemble,
And, like Brigadoon, MLAG appears again
From the planning of many hearts and minds.
And the labor of a year that has passed.
Another June day in Little Buffalo campground
Becomes a time of music and magic.

Out come the folding chairs, the tables,
The sound equipment and the stage.
The backdrop with its window,
The garden fence and arbor
(Harkening back to George's farm where MLAG sank its roots).

The parlor rugs and the plaques of past contest winners.
The Autoharp Hall of Fame reappears in its
accustomed spot,
And another Mountain Laurel begins.

The people, too, begin to gather.
As friends from around the world,
And friends we haven't yet met
Join in a mix of beaming faces.
We've been waiting all year for this moment in time
And there is so much to share.

MLAG is different every time
While the pattern stays the same…
Workshops where sharing newfound talents is the goal,
Concerts with joy hearing new tunes and new players,
Competitions -- where doing well is its own reward,
Jam sessions around the camp – which one to join?
"Air 'Harp" performances – incredible…
Gospel singing, and friendly humor,
A kaleidoscope of sights and sounds,
And far too little sleep.

Suddenly it's Sunday afternoon once again.
The last note of the concert has died away
And the trucks pull up once more to the open door.
We stack the folding chairs and tables in their carts.
Down come the stage lights,
The sound equipment is replaced in its special boxes.
In an hour or so we're back again to an empty room.
MLAG is packed away until next year.

But…it's not the building, not the tents, or the stage.
It's not the stuffed peacock on his throne.
(That's a longer story – you'd have to have been there.)
It's not our musical devices of wood and wire.
These are just the instruments that we choose

To express our gratefulness in music and harmony.
When we all stand in a great circle and sing
"Come One, Come All, To the Family Reunion",
And leave the echoes and the memories here For next year.

Finding the Third Way

My friend, Edwina Goodhue, inspired this poem. We were discussing learning how best to use new computer applications, but the metaphor extends to all the processes in our lives. There is always more than one way to get something done. Thanks, Edwina.

Thanks, too, to Teal Sallen for her illustration of this poem. Teal says "This poem evokes in my mind the image of the first card in the tarot: the fool. The fool is not really an idiot. He is an archetypal fearless seeker and lighthearted explorer out to discover whatever there may be. He is open to inspiration, and not afraid to try something new and innovative, even if it looks crazy. In other words, he pretty much lives for the third way. This lesson is so pivotal that the tarot deck is often said to tell his story, called "the fools journey" ".

*The symbol at the top of the illustration is called an "Awen". In the Welsh tradition, **awen** is the inspiration of the poet bards; or, in its personification. **Awen** is the inspirational muse of creative artists in general: the inspired individual is described as an awenydd.*

"Where there's a will, there's a way"
States the common wisdom.
With sufficient diligence comes success,
And with enough determination,
We reach our goals.

And yet…
Once we've found that one way,
Is that the end of it?
All too soon, our achievement becomes a habit,
An unthinking rut with nothing beyond,

If we have only one way to go.
To grow, we must seek another path,
A second way.

And then…
Once we find that there are more ways
That lead to our desired place.
The branching road becomes an end in itself
And a source of joy we weren't even looking for.

"Seek and you shall find" Is a better approach to life.
Keep on -- ever seeking
To grow, experience, expand, and thrive.
Searching for new ways…
And you <u>will</u> find!

THE THIRD WAY

Missing the Mark

This poem is a commentary on the Hebrew word 'cheyt' (rhymes with 'hate'). Thanks to Ivan Stiles for his illustration of this poem.

The Hebrew word 'cheyt' appears repeatedly
In the liturgy of Yom Kippur.
Usually translated as 'sin',
It suggests a terrible deed
Requiring redemption
And atonement.

Yet, the word itself has ancient Semitic origins
In the field of archery (of all things).
You pick up a bow and draw back the string
Aim at your target, and let your arrow fly.

But…sometimes the arrow goes wide of the target.
You miss the mark, failing to achieve your end.
This is the deeper meaning of 'cheyt'.
The difference – you have more arrows in your quiver.
You can try again.

Bay of Naples

Thanks to Teal Sallen for her beautiful illustration.

Silver filigree runs down to the beach
While sunlight glints off villas and cliffs
Into the Bay of Naples
Capri
Like a cameo against cloud and sea.

Olive groves make a mosaic against the hills
While lemon trees stud the valley
With jewels among the leaves.

Death Without a Casserole

Thank you to Marilee Mansfield, whose marvelous metaphor for divorce inspired me to write this poem. Thanks to Teal Sallen for her artwork.

You left
Just for a little while,
And when you came back
We tried to take up just where we had been,
But you weren't the same.

And you left again....
Longer this time,
And I really missed you
But your letters sounded happy
When you described the new place
Where I wasn't there.

The connections we had together
No longer come to visit.
Some joined your new life
And others just feel too uncomfortable
To spend much time in your empty space.

The person that was our marriage
Died without a funeral,
No flowers and no casket,
No singing and no wake,
No covered dishes brought by friends,
And only one mourner.

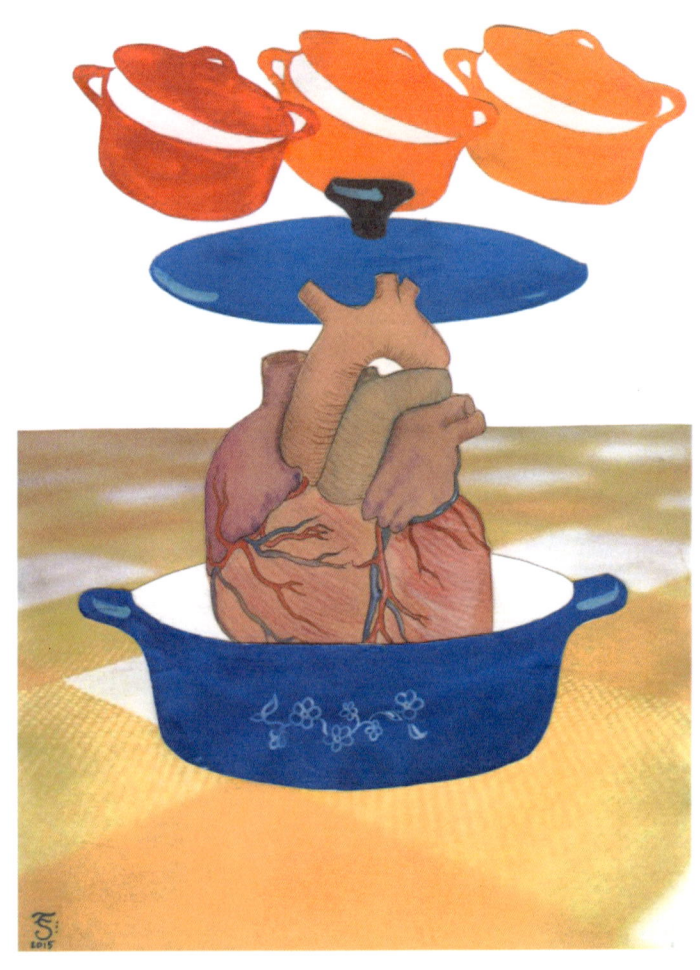

Birthday Present

For twenty-six years
On my birthday
I've received the same present.
Its price is incalculable.
Its wrapping's remarkable,
Too heavy to be portable,
Yet I carry it daily in my heart.

It lasts with care across the years.
I water it with a splash of love
And it feeds my soul (and stomach too).
It carries me beyond my senses
And expands to fill my whole world.
It takes me to new places
And I don't even have to leave home.

Thank you, Lynda, light of my life.

Getting Off the Train

Thank you, cousin Sammy, for inspiring this poem. Also,
thanks to Ivan Stiles for his illustration of this poem.

When I was a child I sat between my parents on the train.
Dad was on my right next to the window,
And my mother was on the aisle, holding my hand.
They were my whole world
And everything I knew ended at the next seat back.

The years passed, and my world enlarged
To include my aunt three rows ahead in her flowered hat,
And the conductor with his brass buttons and shiny ticket punch.
I could see the whole car now
And glimpse the world rushing along outside the window.

Now I'm older still and we walk through the station,
With crowds of people from other trains.
There are sights and sounds, languages and smells
That do not remind me of home.
Where are all these people going?
What do they see outside their train windows?

Today I walk along a city street
Full of tall buildings and green parks.
Bustling sidewalks in a world that teems with life.
And I remember when I thought the whole world
Was contained in a single row of seats
In a single car
On a single train.

How small our worlds would be
If we did not recognize that we are all connected.
Life doesn't end with our seat row (family),
Or our train car (tribe),
Or our train itself (nation).
No, not even at the central station,
Or that one city that is my personal destination.

We must see that all the trains reach their stops,
That every family gets home safely,
That every child sharing a seat with his parents
Is just one of us on the train.

My Eruv

Jewish law requires that no work be done on the Sabbath. However, what is to be defined as "work"? Clearly, pushing a wheelbarrow is work, but what about pushing a baby carriage? What about assisting someone in a wheelchair – is that work or doing a kindness? Carrying a load of bricks is work, but what about an armful of prayer books? This concept of 'work' can get quite slippery.

Over time, the Rabbis developed the concept of "Eruv" – a boundary within which certain acts that would otherwise be considered 'sinful' could be performed without violating one's Sabbath rest. This surrounding wall – physical or imagined – defined the safe limits of the Jewish community. Whether applied from the outside or established from within, the Eruv both shelters and excludes – protects and restricts.

In this poem, I use the idea of the "Eruv" as a metaphor for the boundaries we tend to set around our lives. I'm also using the image of the Venn diagram. Thanks to Teal Sallen for her illustration of this poem.

I had erected an Eruv around my life.
A set of walls and fences within which I felt secure
No places to lose myself
Or stray too far from the safe and familiar.
Nothing too scary – few sleepless nights
A pleasant, well-tended garden

With no unknowns, and few surprises.

One night at M.I.T. your world intersected mine.
We shared some square dances
And some steps beyond our comfort zones
We walked together past the edges of our manicured lawns
Into wild places where our hearts beat faster.
We walked together under starry skies
And saw the sunrise over unfamiliar horizons.

In time, our intersection has formed a union
"Yours" and "mine" become "ours".
You have learned the autoharp
And I pick wild mushrooms.
You use terms like "data points"
And I hike in the woods
(Well, walk a trail somewhat uphill).

Our world together is larger than ever
As we each grow – both inwardly and out.
Limits become places to explore.
And boundaries for one
Are opportunities for sharing

The message – you don't need a wall.
What it keeps out is far more valuable
Than what it holds in.
The risks, the challenges out there at the edge
Are what make us who we can become.

Ordinary Things

This poem was written in remembrance of the 10th anniversary of the September 11 attacks on the World Trade Center. In a smaller way, it also marks the 10 years since my cancer surgery. The poem was inspired by a talk that was given by the New York City fire chief about that fateful day.

Walking across a street,
Climbing a flight of stairs,
Looking out a window,
Opening a door,
Ordinary things.

But when the air is choked with smoke and dust
When glass shards rain like hail from darkened skies
With hundreds trapped in a blacked-out stairwell
These things make men heroes.

Hannibal's Elephants

This poem was written during the Mountain Laurel Autoharp Gathering (MLAG) cruise from Barcelona, Spain, to Ft. Lauderdale, Florida in 2014. To quote the Bill Staines song: "We are crossing the water our whole lives through…to find a peaceful harbor on that far-off shore". Thanks to Ivan Stiles for his illustration of this poem.

I walked behind Hannibal's elephants
Up the shore from Cartagena
Twenty-three centuries too late
To join his army.

I climbed the ramparts of Malaga
The tourist elevator far safer
Than a scaling ladder.
The sounds of street musicians
And a passing bus
Softer than the crash of Spanish artillery.

I sailed through the pillars of Hercules
At Gibraltar, I left the "Middle of the Earth"
(Mediterranean)
And looked out across a fog-shrouded sea.

I travelled with Ponce de Leon
Seeking a fountain of youth
In a new world to the west.

My ship was bigger,
I had better food and a more comfortable bed
As we sailed out over a threatening ocean
Towards a far-off golden shore.

The story of human history
Has a record for us all.
Great king or passing tourist,
We each leave our entries,
Our pages in the book of life.
This poem is one of mine.

Ballad of the MLAG 2006 Alaskan Cruise

*This poem was written about the Mountain Laurel Autoharp Gathering (MLAG) cruise in Alaska in 2006. It is based on a melody "borrowed" from **The Train To Morrow**.*

We started on this journey, about a week ago
To a little town called Juneau, in the state of Alaska-oh
Now I've never been on this cruise before,
So I really didn't know
That MLAG is the finest trip you've ever tried to go.
We went down to Pier 30, bags and 'harps in hand.
We climbed aboard and settled in,
Our gallant little band.
At 3:15 we had the boat drill – at 4:09 we sailed.
'Twas Monday, May the seventh,
The first day of our tale.

We sailed north from Seattle,
Across the sea for Glacier Bay.
Captain Keijer ordered "full ahead",
It was a bright and pleasant day.
With one full day of sailing we spent the eighth of May.
With workshops and late-night jamming,
We whiled the time away.
The ocean waves began to build
Full fifteen feet and more.

Near half stayed in their cabins,
And fondly dreamed of shore.
Others ate a gourmet dinner
Watched the ship's main show
With another half-day of sailing – 300 miles to go.

The seas became much calmer
As we entered Glacier Bay.
The sights were just magnificent
Even though the clouds were gray.
Such mountains, rivers, sea, and sky
What more is there to say!
We spent the whole time marveling until the close of day.
We saw the glaciers calving – icebergs and sea life too
Sipping pea soup, tea, and toddies – and took pictures quite a few.
At 9 PM again we sailed away – to Juneau we did roam.
Aboard the good ship Westerdam that had become our home.

Safely docked in Juneau, next day 'twas spent in port.
With shore tours and excursions
And adventures of all sorts.
Some visited Mendenhall Glacier,
On the ice they did cavort
While others used the spas on ship
Just like a fine resort.
We went out on a whale watch
Saw orcas and humpbacks too.
Sea lions sunning on a buoy – a rainbow's vivid hue.
Then back again we rambled
Ate another real fine dinner,
Another night of jamming – this cruise it was a winner.

We arrived next morn at Sitka
Anchored there offshore.
We tendered in on little boats and there began our tour.
Sitka was a Russian town, with long history and more.
Far too soon we had to leave again – our ship must leave its moor.
Overnight we sailed to Ketchikan

A wondrous little stop.
With totem poles, lumberjack shows,
And every kind of shop.
Another filling dinner – another late-night jam.
Sleeping? Who has time for it? We'll fit it in if we can!

Our last stop was Victoria,
On the Canadian western shore.
The bus was waiting at the dock,
And we began our tour.
The tour guide's name was Norman,
He hailed from London town.
He filled our time with stories
Showed places of renown.
We toured Abkhazi Garden
What a sight it was to see
With bright colors blooming everywhere
Flowers on every tree.
We stopped to hear a pipe band
Their music it was grand
Then back to the ship we hurried
And again we left the land.

So, now we're back in Washington,
Our cruising it is done.
Our bags all packed we disembark at the rising of the sun.
Perhaps we'll meet again at MLAG,
Where again we'll have such fun.
We'll share our pictures, tell our tales, to each and everyone.
So, here's to Shirley Averett and the whole
Cruisewomen crew.
Who organized this trip for us
Did all they could do.
So if next year you have the chance
To take the MLAG tour.
It'll be a great experience, of that you can be sure.

Quantum Scheduling

A question frequently asked in Jewish congregations as September rolls around is, "Are the Holidays early or late this year?". The answer, of course, is that the Holidays are exactly when they're supposed to be – neither early nor late. It's our own schedules that are erratic. The connection to quantum physics came, somehow, from my imagination. I was reminded of the saying "Anyone who claims to understand quantum mechanics does not understand quantum mechanics!" Thanks to Teal Sallen for her illustration (the Schrodinger's paradox familiar from quantum mechanics).

The Rabbi's tell a story about Psalm 81.
The angels in Heaven ask God,
"When is the time to celebrate the New Year?"
And God is said to have replied,
"Go down to Earth and ask my people.
For when they freely choose to honor My commandments,
That is the proper time for rejoicing."

Quantum mechanics states that an electron is both a particle and a wave,
Or, perhaps, neither – it all depends.
Only after a physicist performs a careful experiment,
And observes the nature of reality
Does the electron choose to be a particle or a wave,
Or, perhaps, both.

One view of quantum mechanics believes that there
are 'hidden variables'
That the 'truth' of reality lies beyond the reach of experiment.
We cannot know what the electron really is,
But only how it behaves under certain conditions.

Life is not like this
We have been told what is just and right.
The variables are not hidden
They lie plainly in our sight.
Some people count ten of them
Some a few more or less.
But when we all choose to honor and obey God's laws
of nature
Then the angels in Heaven will celebrate a New Year
And the people of Earth will live in peace.

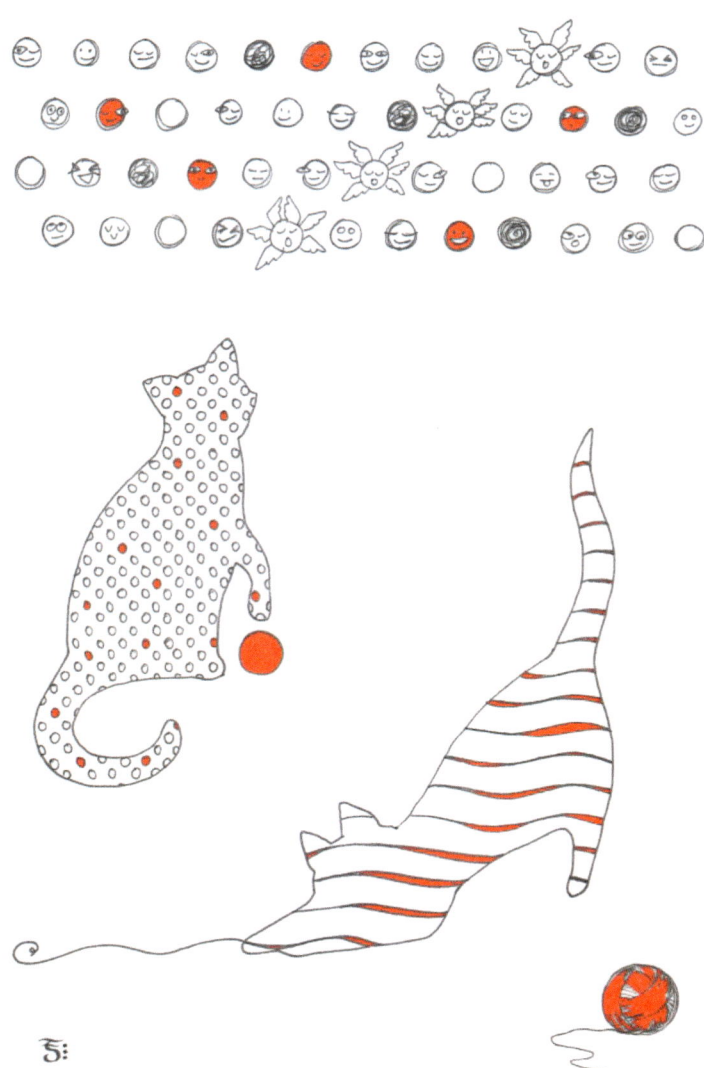

The Aspects of God

It is said that one can determine the things that a people hold important by how many ways they can express it in their language – like how the Eskimos have dozens of terms for various types of snow. If this is so, then the Jewish people must truly find the concept of "deity" important in their lives, for Hebrew has many terms for the varied ways we perceive God.

"No, your Honor" to the judge at traffic court
"Yes Sir, General", when I gave my briefing to the Air Force
"May I have the floor, Mr. Chairman?" at the
international conference
"Your Highness" if I ever meet a king
"Good morning, Father" to the chaplain at M.I.T.
"Hi, Dad" when he came home from work
"How are you doing?" to a good friend
"I do" to my wife at our wedding
"I still love you" after a bitter fight
And to the One who knows my innermost thoughts
There are no words at all.

Manzanar

My good friend, Midori Hall, brought this dark bit of American history to my attention. Midori lived through this period during WWII, when what was "American" came to be questioned. Manzanar was one of the "relocation camps" built to isolate American citizens of Japanese ancestry. We can only hope that our nation is wiser and more inclusive today. Thanks to Teal Sallen for her illustration of this poem. The background to this illustration is the actual plot-plan of the Manzanar relocation camp.

The Paiute Indians farmed this land
Long before the white man came.
The Spanish called it "Manzanar",
The "apple orchard".
Strange – for the apple tree is not native
Transplanted here by European settlers,
Yet "American as apple pie".

In 1861 the U.S. Army drove the Indians from this valley
Along their "Trail of Tears" to Fort Tejon in California.
Cattle ranchers replaced the Indian farmers
And, in 1910, the town of Manzanar was founded.
Orchards were planted, flowers grew,
And the land was fertile.

By 1929 the water had left this place
Pumped away to thirsty Los Angeles.

The orchards and the farms turned to vacant dirt.
Towns and ranches all abandoned.

Far across the sea
"Sakura", the cherry blossoms,
Symbol of ancient Japan
Were not native to the home islands,
But imported from the snowy Himalayas.
The "Ohka", another kind of cherry blossom,
A suicide weapon, born of desperation,
Grew for a time in the same soil.

In 1942, a new crop grew in Manzanar,
Not apple trees, but concrete and barbed wire.
Ten thousand Americans were forced to live here
Because they were not "native".
To endure hardship and shame
For the "crime" of being transplanted.

We won the war in 1945.
The people of Europe were free again,
The concentration camps were liberated.
Manzanar was closed and its inhabitants
Were forced to go their own way.
The barbed wire rusted and the concrete crumbled.
The land was vacant again.

So…we must remember always
Treblinka and Babi Yar, Auschwitz and Manzanar,
We are all transplants, nomads, and mixtures.
Who is "native" to a certain place
Depends mostly on when you ask.

The Laws of Love

You can do anything you want.
There are no rules, no restrictions...
I don't care.
You can have complete freedom.

Well... actually...
I do have one requirement.
Don't do anything that hurts me.
If you're not sure what that might be,
We'll work it out as it comes.

There's just a bit more.
Don't hurt my friends or my neighbors
Because I care for them
Almost as much as I care for you
Or myself.

This is getting complicated!
What about my neighbors' friends?
Where does the circle end?

I'll just have to simplify things for you.
Do not hurt anyone.
Love your neighbor as yourself.
All the rest is commentary,
Worthy of your study.

God Said – And It Was

This poem contrasts the Biblical view with that of the scientist. In many ways, they are just different ways of expressing the same ideas.

In the beginning, did God say
(According to the physicist, Maxwell),
"The divergence of the magnetic field shall be zero"?
And light began to propagate in the newborn universe.

Did God say
(According to the physicist, Bethe),
"Four hydrogen atoms shall fuse to form one of helium,
Releasing energy"?
And formations of stars sparkled across the void.

Did God say
(According to the biologist, Darwin),
"Nature shall evolve and new life grow
As mutation and change in the warmth of starlight"?

Did God say
(According to the zoologist, Linnaeus),
"Let every creature of the sea and bird of the air
And all living things have a name"?
So each Adam and Eve looked out across the Eden that
was theirs,
And it was, indeed, very good.

God did say
(According to His prophet, Moses),
"Here are ten laws for upright living in My world".
And a people camped at the foot of a mountain
Became a nation and a "light to the world"
When they responded, "We will obey."

The Logic of Terrorism

I am often amazed at the ability of many people to hold faithfully to conflicting ideas simultaneously. Thanks to Ivan Stiles for his illustration of this poem.

My life is worth nothing by itself.
Your life is worth nothing by itself.
Only our cause is worthy of dying.

Our God is great.
Our God is merciful.
Our God created all living things.

There is only one God.

What is wrong with this picture?

Redemption

Many people believe that the redemption of the world comes at a far-off time by means of a "magical" divine intervention. However, the Bible and history argue that this is not the case. Humanity has been redeemed many times – and usually by the actions of a few normal people acting in special ways.

Adam and Eve sinned
And the world was no longer a garden.
But their children populated the world,
And we are all their family.

God gave Noah the "rainbow sign"
When a great flood cleansed their sinful world.
The crew of the Ark started over,
And Noah was our father.

Moses led his people out of Egypt
And turned a band of slaves into a nation.
They crossed a sea and wandered a desert
To become a "light to the nations".

The first Temple in Jerusalem was destroyed
Not a stone left on stone.
Ezra and Nehemiah led the exiles back to the land
Where they rebuilt what had been lost.

Rome destroyed the second Temple.

Only the Western Wall was left as a remembrance.
The exiles scattered again among the nations
Where they kept their faith alive.

Six million of us died in the Holocaust.
Millions more lie uncounted around the world.
Yet the nation of Israel prospered
As a blossom grows from barren ground.

So do not ask "whence comes my redemption?"
You have been given so many examples.
We must make of the world a garden
And return to where we started.

The Genesis of the "Big Bang"

The Bible begins the Book of Genesis with the words, "First God made heaven and earth. The earth was without form and void, and darkness was upon the face of the deep…" Modern astrophysics employs the "big bang" theory to describe a not very dissimilar process of universal creation.

"In the beginning" the Biblical universe is formless
No objects, no structures, no rays of light.
To physics, the Big Bang begins in a homogeneous and isotropic plasma soup
With no matter yet formed, all of nature melded into an unknowable lump.
What formed the initial singularity?

And God said, "Let there be light."
In the tiniest fraction of a second,
The plasma universe begins to inflate and cool.
The constituent elemental particles of matter can be born,
Electromagnetism separates from the forces of atomic dimension,
And the first cosmic microwaves race to fill the new space.

"And there was evening and there was morning,
The first day."

A few minutes into the Big Bang,
The universe has the density of air.
After 400 millennia, the first atoms come into being.

Gravity begins to form hydrogen into stars,
And all that we see in the vast heavens has its beginning.

And God said,
"Let there be a firmament in the midst of the waters."
And God called the firmament 'Heaven'.
Lumps in the newly created matter gather together into
the first galaxies.
Over billions of years the process continues,
Until the world of physics is seen by the first human eye.

And God saw everything that He had made, and behold,
it was very good.
And there was evening and there was morning,
A sixth day.

Here we stand today
Whether 6 thousand or 6 trillion years from creation.
Arguing about the time scale
The exact dimensions of the miraculous,
Who or what stirred that initial soup into being,
And whether it is still "very good".

My First Solo

Growing up is a series of small events that eventually result in big changes in one's life. This poem describes one of mine.

It was a weekly family ritual
For as long as I can remember
First thing every Sunday
Dad would drive the five miles to the drugstore on
Main Street
To pick up a copy of the New York Times that was
being held for him.

When he got home we'd distribute the sections.
Dad started with the "News of the Week" and then
"Business".
Mom read the "Book Review" section and the "Arts" pages.
I usually got the "Sports" page first.
But the "Magazine" section we read together...
And doing the crossword puzzle was always a joint effort.

Mom usually started the puzzle by herself.
She'd ask me for help when she got stuck on a clue,
Then Dad helped us to finish it.
I looked forward to doing that puzzle every week.
We all enjoyed the mind stretching,
The wordplay
The anagrams and the puns.
(I still do!)

One Sunday after I had turned sixteen
And had my new driver's license (I was so proud),
Dad handed me his keys and said,
"Go get the paper". I drove so carefully
It might have been faster to ride my bike.
This was the first time I'd ever driven a car without a
co-pilot along.
Homeward I came, turning left onto Melwood Drive,
And looked into our empty garage.

I remember the odd sensation as vividly today
As it was to me nearly a half-century ago.
Where did Dad go?
A missing car meant a missing father,
But that is another story.

It was a little thing
Barely 10 miles, and 30 minutes total.
Yet that moment has always stuck with me,
The feeling of Dad's trust in me
One step along the way to being seen as an equal.
When I'd get to do that Sunday crossword puzzle
On my own.

Raw Materials

There is a liturgical poem in the Jewish Yom Kippur service that compares God's relationship to humanity with the relationship between an artisan and his raw materials – clay and the potter, iron and the blacksmith, glass and the blower, silver and the jeweler, cloth and the draper. This poem is a modern scientist's take on this same idea. Thanks to Teal Sallen for her illustration of this poem.

What is humanity that You are mindful of us?

I'm composed of sixty-five percent oxygen,
About 100 pounds of colorless gas,
As free as the air we breathe,
Combined with hydrogen making water
Not enough to fill an average bathtub.

I'm twenty-eight pounds of carbon
Born in the heart of a dying star.
I'm the ashes of a stellar fire,
Enough for a good barbecue
Or a funeral pyre.

I'm sixteen pounds of hydrogen,
The first element created in the "Big Bang"
In the beginning, God...
The fuel of young stars.

Nitrogen and calcium make about eight pounds
Of star-stuff and my bones.
Part of my body made in a violent supernova
And good for fertilizer.

Alkali metals make up less than a pound of me.
Potassium, sodium, rubidium...
Worth about 140 dollars in today's market
Valuable not because of rarity,
But because they're hard to extract
From the dust of the Earth.

That leaves just four pounds of me
For everything else in the periodic table.
Iron and gold, sulfur and silver,
Copper, uranium, chlorine, platinum...
Stuff both scarce and commonplace,
Reactive and inert
Cheap and expensive,
I would not live without them all.

The Stream of Tradition

I attended an interesting Bar Mitzvah service last Saturday morning. Three generations of our family shared the coming-of-age ceremony of the new generation. Ancient words of prayer were set to new melodies. Centuries-old traditions were combined with modern sensibilities. As one of my cousins remarked, "We are each the product of our moment in time."

This poem is structured in sets of four – reminding me of the incessant 4/4 beat of the music at the Bar Mitzvah party on Saturday night.

I walked beside a glistening stream on a summer's day
Gravel crunching beneath my feet as sunlight danced
on the water.
A mossy boulder left frothy rapids on its downstream side,
A nearly uprooted tree trailed its branches along the stream bank,
And a fish jumped to capture a fly from the mirrored surface.

I do not know the source of this stream
Hundreds of miles north in craggy mountains
Winter snow-melting.
I do not know its ending miles southeastward
Past sleepy mill towns through a bustling harbor
And out into the open sea.

I do not know this stream in a thunderstorm's violence
Rain splashing, lightning flashing, thunder booming.

I do not know this stream in the depth of winter
Icy sheet over the water, drifts of new snow,
And stillness where once was burble and windy sigh.

I only know this stream as it appears today
Warm sunshine, sparkling water, and that fish.
Postcard beauty leaves an image in my heart.
When again I return to this stream in my memory
It will always be this setting that I see.

The Plastic Christmas Tree

Last week I attended a very unusual Bat Mitzvah – an entire Sabbath service with not one mention of God. No "Shema", no "Kaddish", no "Amidah" and no call to communal prayer. There was a reading from Torah, whose first words are "In the beginning, God…", yet nothing was said about who commanded us to rest on the "seventh day". The occasion felt vaguely odd and detached – all form and no substance. This poem expresses my feelings about the experience. Thank you to Ivan Stiles for his illustration of this poem. Also, thank you to Teal Sallen for her collage.

There is a plastic Christmas tree down at the mall
Every needle a perfect green.
Untouched by winter wind or early frost,
Summer's heat or parching drought,
It stands with ideal symmetry among the shoppers
Lost in their own and personal worlds.
Unnoticed, the sounds of recorded carols
Mix with scents from the food court.

This tree has never felt a squirrel's foot,
Or sheltered a blue jay,
Or fed a foraging deer.
This tree was never part of a forest.
No community of Nature here.
No drops of amber resin, no scent of pine,
No growth, no decay, no death,
Only a never-changing present.

This tree wears decorations of mylar tinsel
In the image of frozen icicles,
Sprayed-on imitations of the winter's depth.
There is no indication here of season's turning
No December cold about to yield to life's rebirth,
No rising sun, no deep snow stillness,
No connection to timeless cycles.

This tree is hung with glass balls reflecting in the floodlights
Fragile, like the present – so easy to break
Mirroring the world around them,
Glittering like Heaven's stars
But with no warmth of their own to share.

The gift-wrapped boxes piled beneath this tree
Hold no fresh new joys to discover.
There will be no shouts of elation as these ribbons are removed.
January turning to April will bring no new life,
No promise of fragrant flowers
Or the warmth of a blooming summer.

In a short few weeks they'll take down this plastic tree.
It's served its purpose here, no need to linger.
They'll come and put away all the decorations and the tinsel,
The gift boxes placed back on their seasonal shelves,
The green plastic branches stored in cardboard boxes,
And this tree will disappear.

For Ivan

Ivan Stiles has been my musical mentor and a good friend for many years. His instrumental and artistic virtuosity are exceeded only by his warmth, humility, and sense of humor. This poem, Ivan, is for you. Thank you for the illustration.

The Bible says,
"You shall not use implements of iron in service to the Temple.
Tools of warfare cannot be used to praise the name of God."
The Levites never heard Ivan play the saw!

A simple sheet of steel Held in tension
Out of its comfort zone
To produce such wonderful sounds.
A wail of pain – a moan of delight,
A lover's sigh,
Drawn forth by the stroke of his bow.

For if, indeed, Angels can dance
On the head of a pin
Then a heavenly choir stands arrayed
Along the edge of your saw blade.

For you, Ivan,
God has made an exception.

The Teacher

This poem was derived from the book <u>Decoded,</u> written by Mai Jia. It describes the emotions felt at that 'aha' moment when the student- teacher relationship changes to that of partner and colleague. Richard Scholtz read us this passage during the introduction to Seattle Autoharp Week (SAW) in 2014. Thanks to Richard, Bryan, Karen, and Cathy (the SAW instructors) who are the flame that drew so many of us to the autoharp. Thanks, too, to Ivan Stiles and Teal Sallen for their illustrations of this poem.

You must run, hard and fast
Down narrow trails and across broad fields.
I will chase you as fast as you will let me.
I will be the spark – the flame at your back.
But, if you stop running and I catch you,
The lesson is over.

Yet, if you run so fast and far
That all I can see is your glow
Brilliant against the night sky.
The lesson, too, is over.

So…run as hard and fast as you can.
Thus begins the lesson.

Dot the Dragon's Eyes

This poem is based upon an old Chinese metaphor for that magical final step in the process when mere 'artifice' becomes 'art' – the transcendence of the mere physical world and its limitations. I heard violinist, Hanneke Cassel, play her piece with this title at a concert today, and this poem was a result.

I want to thank my cousin, Teal Sallen, for her fantastic illustration to this poem. Historically, the dragon was the symbol of the Emperor of China. In the Zhou Dynasty, the 5-clawed dragon was assigned to the Son of Heaven, the 4-clawed dragon to the nobles, and the 3-clawed dragon to the ministers. In the Qin Dynasty, the 5-clawed foot dragon was assigned to represent the Emperor while the 4-clawed and 3-clawed dragons were assigned to the commoners. Thanks, Teal, for your 5-clawed artwork!

An aged Chinese painter sits before his drawing table,
A clean sheet of rice paper, open to all inspiration.
He looks into his soul, a brush in his hand.

A scaly tail takes shape – green with golden flecks.
Sinuously, it elongates into a muscular body
With leathery wings held taut by a skeleton of unseen bone.

Ivory talons appear, red-tinged with deadly curve
As if clinging to the very paper on which they are drawn.
The huge mouth filled with fierce pointed teeth.

The artist stops to inspect his painting.
The dragon's eyes are blank and featureless.
There is only potential here.

Two dots of paint complete the eyes.
The dragon glares deeply into your soul and roars.
The artist is very pleased.